Contents

Jogging

Chapter One

"Your tennis has got better, Jeff. But if you don't get faster before March, you haven't got much of a chance," my tennis coach, Mr Allen, told me with a friendly smile. That was last October on the last day of tennis practice. Then I knew that I had to jog every day if I wanted to be a member of the tennis team at our high school in the summer.

My hobbies are tennis, skate-boarding and I play the piano. Mike, my best friend, and I skate-board in a quiet street near my house. Mike is a year younger than I am, but he's really good at skate-boarding. That's the only thing he can do

better. Mike lives in our street. He's lucky because he has only one older brother who doesn't bother him much. I have a bratty eight-year-old sister, Barbara, or Babs as her friends call her, who's my mother's favourite. My father is away on business a lot, but I think Babs makes him nervous, too. The problem with our neighbourhood is that there are a lot of little kids around. But all my friends except Mike live near the high school. Sometimes I go over there with the new motorcycle I got for my sixteenth birthday. Mike and I often play tennis at Milford Park or mow lawns for our lawn-mowing business.

I'm in the tenth grade at the high school in Milford. School is boring most of the time. Mike goes to private school now, so he isn't even on my bus any more. My father says I could get good grades if I worked harder, so it isn't worth sending me to private school. I wanted to go to our high school anyway, because I have a chance of getting on the tennis team there. And a lot of kids I like very much also go to the high school, like Lucy Smith. She has been in my class since kindergarten.

So in October I started jogging. My route went into town, back a longer way behind our house and home again. At first I always took about forty-five minutes to run the route. Of course, it was difficult to leave the house. My mother always wanted to know where I was going. She was frightened when I told her my jogging route. She was afraid for me in the traffic, at night and in the cold. My bratty sister always wanted to come with me and shouted when I told her she couldn't. Then, once I was finally on my way, it was really hard. For the first few runs I had to concentrate on my breathing. After the first two weeks, I could sometimes look at the shop windows in town. I was a little more careful at the traffic lights. I often looked into our neighbours' gardens and houses when I came to that part of my route.

There are always some houses for sale in our neighbourhood, and the one on Duncan Street was also on my route. I started to watch all the changes in town, especially in our own neighbourhood, during my jog. Soon I saw a change at that same house every Wednesday. And it wasn't people interested in buying the house or moving in.

Usually the house was empty and dark, and nobody was near it or in it. No cars were parked anywhere near the house. But every Wednesday a wine-red Ford was in the driveway of the house and somebody was working in the garden. The Ford didn't really look like a normal gardener's van. But maybe it belonged to the owner of the house or a friend who was doing garden work. When we changed back the clocks and the late afternoons got darker, I saw a light on in a back room. I also saw shadows of people on the back lawn.

I asked myself why the same people met at an empty house every Wednesday evening. They sat in one room and left all the others dark. Repairmen work every day, not just one day a week. I couldn't understand it. The house was in my thoughts all week after I had realized how often this had happened on Wednesdays. I decided to check the house the next week. I didn't like feeling so unsure about it.

The next Wednesday I passed the house again. When I was far enough so the gardener couldn't see me any more, I went around to the back and through the garden behind the house. I was careful. I stayed in the shadows, and I walked up quietly to the back of the house. When I was standing under the window with the light on, I could hear three voices; one gruff, deep man's voice, one girl's voice and one boy's voice, probably about my age. At first I couldn't really understand anything, but soon I could hear some words, "Fifty dollars ... half an ounce ... pure."

I waited quietly and thought about what I had heard. Slowly I understood what was happening, but it was so unlikely in our neighbourhood, that I listened again. This time I clearly heard the word 'coke'. Now I was really sure. There was something going on here with drugs. I moved away quietly and ran home as fast as I could.

When I got home, my mother was nervous because I was fifteen minutes late. I still wasn't sure about what I had heard, so I just ate my meal quickly and went to bed. The strange thing was that I was sure that I had heard one of those voices before. But where, and who was it? And what should I do now? With these questions in my head, I didn't sleep till midnight.

Chapter Two

In school the next day, I was thinking about what had happened the day before. I couldn't listen to the teachers. Of course, I had to go to the police about my discovery – that was clear. But would they believe me, a sixteen-year-old? Or should I tell my father the story? No, that wasn't a good idea; he was always tired and nervous after work. I had to do it myself. I was thinking about this when my English teacher asked a question. Then I heard something that made me think of the house. I heard the same voice that I had heard at the house. I looked around and saw it was Lucy Smith. She was answering the English teacher's question.

I felt myself turn white, then red, then white and cold. I just couldn't believe it. Lucy Smith involved in drugs? A nice girl like Lucy? Now I had to go to the police. Right after school. I didn't want Lucy to be involved in drugs. It was even more terrible than I had thought.

So I got off the bus in town near the police-station. I hadn't thought about the last part of the journey home. I felt quite sure of myself, as I went into the police-station next to the library. A tall police officer was sitting at a desk. He didn't look up when I came in, so I said, "Good afternoon." The policeman was still writing, but at last he looked up.

"Good afternoon, can I help you?" he asked in a bored voice.

"Yes, I think there are drug dealers in an empty house in Duncan Street. They sell their drugs to teenagers there."

"Well, son, what you think isn't enough here. The police have to have some proof. How did you get this idea?"

"The house is usually empty, but every Wednesday a wine-red Ford is in the driveway and somebody works in the garden and ..."

"Haven't you ever heard of a gardener? The owners are probably trying to make a nice garden, so somebody will buy the house at last. Get back to your schoolbooks and your sports, and don't bother us with your teenage fantasies. We have serious work to do here, with real criminals."

"But sir, I'd like to tell you the whole story. I'm sure a drug dealer goes there ..."

"Of course, probably disguised as a gardener, right? Leave their job to the police, son. Now go home and stop wasting time. Your mother is worrying where you are. Goodbye."

And so this bored police officer had laughed at me and I had to walk all the way home and carry my school things.

I started walking. I was tired and thinking about what I could say to my mother when I got there, because I was more than an hour late.

I tried to go in quietly as if nothing had happened, but, of course, Babs shouted and everybody saw me. My parents wanted me to explain why I had missed the bus and why I was so late. I said something about staying after school and then I went up to my room.

After I had done my homework, I had to decide what to do next. The police didn't want to help me, so the only thing I could do was to find out more for myself. But it was too dangerous to check the house and be near the criminals alone, so I had to choose an assistant. The best person was Mike. I was sure he would believe me and help. So I decided to tell him the whole story. The next day I went over to Mike's house and talked about it with him. Mike was even more enthusiastic about it than I was myself.

"Hey, man, that's really terrible. We'll be in the newspapers if we catch that drug ring."

I told him that we didn't know if a whole ring was involved, that we had to have some proof first, and that the whole thing was very frightening. That's when Mike had one of his coolest ideas.

"We have to keep a diary of everything we see that happens at that house. We have to collect really clear evidence," said Mike. He had really understood the idea now. Every Wednesday he jogged with me. After the first time, we decided that Mike should walk down to the corner of Miller Road and Duncan Street to meet me. That first Wednesday he was running so hard he got a stitch and had to walk. Soon, we had an idea about what was happening. We kept careful notes of every new and different thing we saw and all the conversations we heard. Mike was really brave and

went right up to the car sometimes, even when the gardener was there. We found out that he wasn't really a gardener, but that comes later. Here are some of the things we wrote in the diary:

Wednesday, 14th November

1. *Ford in the same place.*
2. *Man with dark beard, brown trousers and dark blue pullover working in the garden.*
3. *Three people in kitchen at the back of house:*
   - *man, about 40, blue and green pullover, jeans;*
   - *girl, it really is Lucy Smith, student at Milford High School;*
   - *boy, about 15, black.*
4. *Together the kids buy two ounces of cocaine for $200.*

5. The man in the kitchen has a big, brown leather bag.
6. Mike goes quietly over to car and sees small brown paper bags under the front seats.

Wednesday, 21st November

1. Wine-red Ford car, gardener and other man with beard arrive at 5:02 pm.
2. Kids are already at the back of house.
3. Man tells gardener to stay near the car – there's a lot of money in there. He leaves car doors open.
4. Gardener has to look after car.
5. Man with beard and kids go in and leave through the back door.
6. Today they buy another two ounces.
7. All leave at 5:39 pm.
8. Two men leave in car, kids leave through garden door.
9. walk behind Lucy as far as her house (109 Miller Road).
10. Mike follows boy to 9 Sycamore Street.

We collected information for over six weeks. Then Mike and I decided it was enough for our plan. Now we had:
- our notes in our diary
- an unclear tape of the voices in the house
- the number of the car
- some wool from the dealer's pullover that he had caught on one wall of the house
- some paint Mike had taken off a dirty place on the car.

Now we were ready. The only problem was to convince the police that it was time to arrest the gang. I was also really worried about what could happen to Lucy; I didn't want her to go to jail ... Our next step was to think of a good plan so that the police could arrest the criminals by surprise. We didn't want them to have a chance to escape after our weeks of work.

Chapter Three

Mike and I both agreed that we needed some of the drug to convince the police to come and arrest the gang. The big problem was to get the man in the garden away from the car. One of us could then take one of the small bags from under the seat. This was the evidence we needed. Mike and I thought about this problem for at least three days. Then one day Mike came over when I was repairing my motorcycle in the garage. He wanted to help me. At last! I knew the best way to take the gardener's eyes away from the car: a 'broken' motorcycle. As soon as I told Mike, he was happy about the idea, too.

Then we started working on the details of our plan. It was clear that I would have to be the 'unlucky' motorcycle owner. I could ask for the gardener's help and talk to him for as long as possible. This was the chance for Mike to get a small bag out of the car, run to the neighbour's house, phone the police and then wait for the officers to arrive. We tried to think of all the details. We wrote a list of the things Mike should tell the police, and the things that he mustn't forget because he was so excited. Some of the things on the list were:

- the police should block the driveway with their car, so that nobody could escape by car
- they should quickly block the back door
- nobody should come over to me.

Mike also had to ask if the police could come in other clothes. Our list also had other information like Mike's name and address and the address of the house. We wanted to stop the motor by blocking the gas with some paper in the filter. And we practised judo in case we had to fight. Our plan was that Mike could get into the car but nobody should see him. Then Mike and I could silence the man in the garden when he saw a strange car in the driveway. And, of course, the most important idea was that the police should come immediately.

The Big Wednesday came. In my thoughts, I repeated what I had to do over and over again. I also thought about all the things that could go wrong. By the time I came home, I had the most terrible pain in my stomach. I was really nervous. I didn't tell my mother why I was going out on my

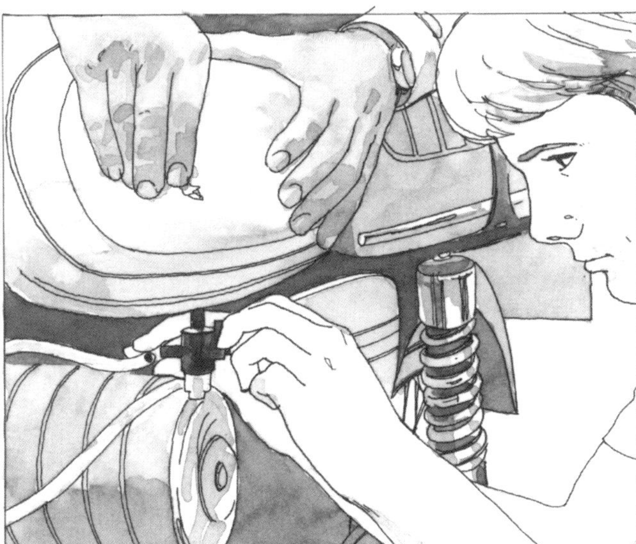

motorcycle and not jogging. Then I went over to meet Mike. He was even more nervous than I was, but everything we did from then on went well.

We started off on my motorcycle and then stopped 200 metres from the Duncan Street house, opened the gas line quickly and put some paper in to clog the filter. We closed it up again and started the motorcycle. Mike got off a few houses before the 'drug' house and I drove on slowly till I was nearly in the garden, away from the driveway, but near enough so the gardener could see me. I was afraid the gas would last too long, but then my motorcycle suddenly stopped and it just didn't start again. I tried to look as worried as possible. I looked at my watch, checked my motorcycle and tried to make it start. At last I got off, pushed the bike off the street and onto the grass. I tried to do everything very slowly to give Mike time. I started to repair my motorcycle, and I felt even more nervous. The gardener just went on with his work. He looked at me quickly now and then. Just when I thought I would have to call and ask for his help, he walked over to me. I tried to look very busy – just repairing my motorcycle.

"Need any help, kid?" a gruff, but not unfriendly voice asked.

I felt as if I was going red, but then I said quietly, "I don't understand it. The motor just stopped, but there's enough gas."

"I know a lot about motorcycles," the man said and smiled. "Perhaps I can repair it for you."

"Yeah," I said. I was hoping that he wouldn't think of the filter immediately. I got out the tool kit and we checked things on the motorcycle. I felt it took a long time. I thought about Mike all the time – would the man hear Mike when he opened the car door? Would he think of the filter, find the paper and the whole plan would go wrong? I was very nervous. To my surprise, the man didn't see how nervous I was or Mike at the car. I was too worried to look up to see what Mike was doing at the car or if he was gone. I tried to be normal on the outside, but a thousand things were jumping around in my head and each minute lasted longer than sixty seconds.

But from the minute I heard Mike, who was whistling as he walked down the street, everything happened quickly. Just as two cars drove up the driveway, Mike walked over to us to 'help' and suddenly put his scarf over the gardener's mouth. Automatically, I got his arms into the grip we had practised while Mike tied the scarf. He helped me take

control of the man, who stood there surprised and helpless. The police were really great. Two police officers came over and took our man. Three other police officers walked up to the back door very quickly and quietly and took the group in the kitchen by surprise. The man with the beard had heard the cars and was just trying to go out the back door, but they arrested him.

We watched the police when they drove away in their cars and the wine-red Ford with the criminals and the kids before we really knew it was all over. Mike and I were really glad – but I felt terrible when I saw Lucy in there with criminals and police officers. We opened the gas line again, took the paper out of the filter, started up my motorcycle and drove to Mike's. I called my mom and told her I was eating dinner at Mike's, so she didn't have to worry. And we sat on the living-room floor and talked through every minute of the last hour to each other till the phone rang. We had to go to the police-station. There we showed what we thought was a very professional book of evidence. They asked us lots of questions. The police congratulated us on a good job.

Just as we wanted to leave, a man came in, who knew everybody. He was the 'Milford News' reporter for police stories. When he learned from the police officer about the gang, we had to tell the story all over again into the microphone of his cassette-recorder and then he took our picture. We were so glad to get out of the police-station that I forgot to ask about Lucy. I thought about it all the way home and decided to tell my parents. My mom wasn't too happy, of course, but she told me not to worry about Lucy; young criminals don't usually go to jail.

Chapter Four

When my dad opened the newspaper the next morning, he got a big surprise. The front page looked like this:

The Milford News

LOCAL BOYS CRACK DRUG RING

The Milford police got help yesterday, when two local boys, Jeffrey Mills, 16, of 10 Lincoln Avenue and Michael Mesiti, 15, of 13 Lincoln Avenue called and told them about strange activities in an empty house in their neighbourhood. The boys saw strangers there for a few weeks and had collected enough evidence to convince the police of criminal activity. The boys were correct: the police confirm that they were trying to find a ring of big city drug dealers in this town. Yesterday they were lucky – thanks to Jeffrey and Michael.

My dad looked up from the newspaper and smiled even though he hadn't finished his first cup of coffee. "I must say, you two, you guys did the right thing," my dad said.

"It was very dangerous," my mother said nervously.

And Babs, her bratty self, said, "You look as if you hadn't washed for a week in that picture." But for once I didn't say anything.

At school I was a real hero; all the teachers and even the head teacher congratulated me, and the guys all cheered. I didn't have to worry about my popularity any more. After school, people even stopped Mike and me on the street in town and said things like, "You're the kid detectives, aren't you?" We felt like a million dollars.

But even with all this, I was still very unhappy about what was happening to Lucy. I heard that she had to go to a special hospital for a few weeks. Then her family was going to have family therapy together after that. So maybe things will be better for her than before she got into trouble.

You know, after all those exciting weeks, I wasn't interested in jogging any more. It just wasn't the same, and there was no reason for Mike to go with me. The jogging was often too much for him. I did try out for the tennis team in the spring, but I only got a place as a substitute. The funny thing is, it isn't important now. When Lucy was in that special hospital, I went to visit her a few times. I even convinced her that it could be fun to play some tennis. So now we often meet for a game of tennis in Milford Park.

Amaryllis on Her Own

Chapter One

Amaryllis walked slowly down the street. She was going to a new place. Her thoughts weren't all happy. All the kids on the street were pleased to see each other. They were making lots of noise. Amaryllis felt even more miserable. She remembered her old home in Waltham, a thousand miles away and her best friend, Jane. Now she felt even sadder than before. What would this school be like? Would she find new friends here?

At last, she saw the sign 'Columbus Junior and Senior High School'. Amaryllis followed the other students into the building. She looked at her timetable one more time to check her homeroom; yes, it was H212. She walked across the courtyard and saw that her new school wasn't that different from her old one. "Maybe all schools are the same," she thought.

Luckily, she soon found H Building. Room H212 was already full of lots of noisy students. They were throwing paper, shouting and laughing. When Amaryllis came in the room was quiet for a minute, and then the noise began again. Amaryllis sat in the second row next to a girl with long blond hair. She smiled and then asked if the seat was free. She could now look around the classroom. The loudest person in the room was a short boy with red hair. He was throwing paper planes and shouting 'pie face' or 'noodle head'. The other students laughed and sent back the planes – and names.
"Who's that boy?" Amaryllis asked her neighbour.
"That's Michael, a terrible show-off," she answered.

"But he's very popular. Everybody just calls him Carrot." There was another person who was throwing almost as many paper planes as Carrot. He was a tall boy who was sitting near a window.
"Who's that?" Amaryllis asked again.
"His name is John. He's really stupid," the blond girl answered.

The noise was getting quieter, when a kid who was at the door said the teacher was coming. Immediately all the paper planes disappeared and everybody sat in their seats. Their homeroom teacher, Mr Mason, came into the classroom. Amaryllis didn't know why, but she didn't like this tall man. He didn't look at the class. He told them to stand and said the Pledge of Allegiance with them in a bored voice. Then he gave the usual beginning-of-the-year talk about working hard, and called their names. Amaryllis was the only new student in the group, and when he called her name, the class giggled. The blond girl next to her was Sandra. When she saw that Amaryllis felt bad, Sandra passed her a note which said, "Don't worry. You can call me Sandy." Amaryllis smiled at her and whispered, "Thanks."

Then Mr Mason said, "Amaryllis, tell the class something about yourself." She felt very hot, but she stood up and said, "I'm Amaryllis Craus, and I'm 15 years old. I have a brother who is nine years old. We moved here from Waltham, near Boston, because the computer company my father works for sent him here. I'm also really interested in computers."
"Fine. Thank you, Amaryllis. You can sit down again now," Mr Mason said. "All of you take out your timetable and see where you have to go for the first lesson."
Amaryllis took out her timetable and read, 'Computer Science 3, Ms Norton, Room G116.' She looked over at Sandra's timetable and saw that she had the same thing. Amaryllis began to feel better. The bell rang. Amaryllis stayed near Sandra and they went downstairs and over to G Building.

When they walked into Room G116, Ms Norton, a young, dynamic-looking woman with a smile, was waiting for them. The other kids already knew her and it was clear that they liked her. After they had listened to a short talk, the class could start the day's exercise. They had to use the program to show the percentage of games the school's sports teams had won and lost in the year before. Ms Norton gave photocopies of all the results.
There were only sixteen computers, so some of the students had to work together. A girl with short, dark hair, Pat, asked

Sandy to work with her. Amaryllis had to share with John. That wasn't great, but at least she knew who he was.

"You work out the number of wins and the number of losses and I'll do the program," John said. Amaryllis wanted to talk about the exercise, because she was sure he would make a mistake. She was right. After three steps, she saw that he had programmed it to show the number of wins and losses as numbers – not as percentages.

"Let me correct something," Amaryllis said. She moved to the computer. She typed in three more steps, but John didn't want them.

"That's all wrong," he said angrily.

"I'm sure it isn't. Ask Ms Norton." So John asked. "Ms Norton, Amaryllis is making mistakes in my program." Amaryllis could hear the giggles and whispers in the room. She felt all the eyes were looking at the back of her head.

Ms Norton spoke clearly to John. "It's her program, too. Now let me have a look at the problem."

Ms Norton looked at the three steps on the screen. "That's very good, Amaryllis, but the others haven't learned such difficult steps. You come to my computer and I'll give you something more difficult to do. John, remember that you should work with percentages."

Amaryllis was pleased that Ms Norton now knew how good her work was, but she was sure John wouldn't forget their first computer lesson together.

Chapter Two

Things got better and better as Amaryllis learned about the different buildings, and found the library books on computers and horses (her two favourite subjects). She found the lunch menu for the next week. In this school she could choose to use her lunch ticket or bring sandwiches each day. She asked Ms Norton if she could do her homework on a computer after school sometimes.

But one Tuesday morning, when Amaryllis walked into her homeroom, she heard the giggles and whispers again. As soon as Sandy arrived, Amaryllis asked her what was wrong. "Pat told me on the bus that somebody saw you in the computer room on Friday after school," Sandy answered.
"Sure. What's wrong with that?" Amaryllis answered. "I was doing my homework."
"The expensive new printer is broken. If you're the last person who worked in that room, then a lot of people will think you did it. They'll probably say you broke it," Sandy said.
"But it wasn't me!" Amaryllis said quickly. "Really, it wasn't!"
"Well, I believe you," said Sandy. "But who else could it be? Nobody is in school on Saturday and Sunday, and on Monday morning it was broken."
Amaryllis felt even sicker to her stomach than she had on that very first day of school. Just then Mr Mason walked in. He was angry and gave the group a talk about how the truth always comes out in the end. He looked right at Amaryllis and so did everybody else, of course. Then he said, "We're sure the guilty person will say what happened. If nobody goes to the head teacher, Mrs Jones, by Thursday, she'll take measures."
Amaryllis was so hot and angry, that she didn't know what to do. Then the bell rang for first lesson. But she didn't have to think for too long, because Mr Mason came over to her.
"I was here after school on Friday. I saw you come out of the computer room. Don't think that we aren't going to find out who broke the printer."
Amaryllis was afraid to answer, because she didn't want to get angry. She just looked at the floor and pushed her way

past Mr Mason out to the hall. She wasn't even sure how she got to G116, but was glad to see Ms Norton. But today, her favourite teacher wasn't friendly. She was very quiet and just gave the class an easy exercise.

The bell rang one last time at the end of a terrible day for Amaryllis. She went back quickly to the computer room, but not to do her homework.

Ms Norton was there, and Amaryllis asked her what was happening.

"Mr Mason thinks I broke something here, and I'm sure I didn't," Amaryllis explained.

"The new printer is broken," Ms Norton said quickly and she didn't look up. Amaryllis couldn't understand why this Ms Norton wasn't like her old friend.

Ms Norton and Amaryllis didn't know what to say next. Before she had a chance, the Computer Science teacher started again.

"Amaryllis, to tell you the truth, my son broke it."

Ms Norton was surprised at herself. She hadn't wanted to say anything, but suddenly it all came out.

"I didn't have time at school to program some new certificates for Games Day. So I just thought I could take the printer home and use it with *my* computer. I wanted those certificates to look really great this year. So I thought I could do it at home at the weekend. I just went into the kitchen to make myself a cup of coffee and my five-year-old son, Douglas, probably broke it by accident. When I got back to the computer, the printer just didn't work. I couldn't see or find anything wrong. I shouted at Douglas, but he didn't say anything. He didn't know what had happened."

Amaryllis was feeling easier now. There was no question any more about who had done it. But why didn't Ms Norton just tell the truth?

"That's too bad, Ms Norton," Amaryllis said, and she tried to think what to say next. Could she criticize a teacher or tell her what to do? She wanted to try to find out more. "Why don't you just take it back to the computer shop? They can repair it there. If it's so new, there's a guarantee on it."

"But Amaryllis," Ms Norton said quietly, "it worked fine before. And if I say that I took it out of the building and I didn't ask Mr Pickering, the department head, he'll be angry. He's going to find out that Douglas played with it. I'm afraid it will look bad on my record."

Amaryllis felt as if she was suddenly in a strange adult world she didn't understand. What record? Teachers don't get reports! Ms Norton answered her question before Amaryllis could ask it.

"This is the second year of my two-year contract. I was new last year, and this year is when I really have to show I can do the job well. The Board of Education will say soon which teachers they're going to keep and which have to leave. Now I just don't know what to do." Ms Norton was nervous and frightened.

Amaryllis didn't know teachers worried so much about their jobs, and she wanted to help Ms Norton if she could. "I think I have an idea, Ms Norton," Amaryllis said. "My father works at a computer company and has the same printer in his department. I've seen it there when we go to meet him sometimes. It looks just the same. Perhaps he could lend us his printer and he can repair this broken one. Or maybe somebody at his company can repair it. Give me your phone number and I'll call you this evening after he comes home from work." Amaryllis was a little surprised herself how all those words came out suddenly, but Ms Norton looked very, very happy.
"That's terrific, Amaryllis! I don't know how to thank you!"
"That's OK, Ms Norton," Amaryllis answered. "It's just something we can try."

Ms Norton gave Amaryllis her phone number and started to organise things.
"If your father brings his company printer home this evening, I'll collect it at your house. Then I can exchange the printers here at school and bring the school printer to your house. Your father needn't drive here."
"Fine, Ms Norton. I'll go home now and call my Dad. Then I'll call you."

Amaryllis and Ms Norton said goodbye and each went home. They were both happier for the first time that day. They didn't know that somebody else was happy but not about the same thing; John was just walking past the open door of G116 on his way to basketball practice when he

heard the conversation behind the door. Now he knew how he could make Amaryllis and Ms Norton feel terrible. He hadn't forgotten that first computer lesson with Amaryllis.

Chapter Three

The first thing Amaryllis did when she got home was to call her father.

"Hello? Fred Craus speaking."

"Daddy, listen. This is an emergency. My teacher's son broke the school's printer. Can you bring your printer home and exchange it with the broken one? Then somebody has got to repair the school's broken printer. You see, Ms Norton is afraid to say she has broken it. Her contract finishes this year and everybody thinks I did it. Please, Daddy," Amaryllis said quickly. Her father laughed, but he tried to understand.

"Well, that's quite a problem. I don't understand it all. But we can talk about it this evening. We use that printer here in the office all the time. Maybe we can go to another department to print our work out for the next few days. I hope it isn't too difficult to find what's broken."

"But you can bring it home, can't you, Daddy?" Amaryllis wanted to be sure.

"All right. I'll bring our printer home this evening. And then I want to hear what happened. Bye." When she had called Ms Norton she felt much better. That evening Mr Craus brought home the company's printer and Ms Norton exchanged it with the school printer. The next morning the school had a laser printer in the computer room. And Mr Craus and his assistant had to find the problem in the broken model as fast as they could.

As Amaryllis fetched her Maths book from her locker between the third and fourth lesson that same morning, she felt happy as could be. Oh, this was going to be a surprise for Mr Mason. She walked quickly to the classroom for Maths, but she stopped outside the door when she heard her name.

"Amaryllis is really in trouble now. I'm going to tell Mr Mason about Ms Norton and how Amaryllis is helping her. She'll really be in trouble then." It was John, and it was clear to Amaryllis that he knew everything.

"Don't be silly. Just because she's so much better at computers than you are and you're angry. Do you really want Ms Norton to leave? Don't you remember – she was the only teacher who wanted to take us on that bike trip to the lake last year?" said Sandy in a strong voice.

"And Ms Norton really makes computers much more fun than old Pickering! It's going to be terrible if she has to leave! If Amaryllis can do something so Ms Norton can stay here, that's fine. She's great to try like that and not just criticize Ms Norton. Just because you're so bad at Computer Science, John, that doesn't mean all the class has to hate Amaryllis,"said Carrot.

"Amaryllis is the nicest girl in the class. She's only trying to help one of our favourite teachers. We should try to help her," he said.

Sandy felt stronger when she knew Carrot agreed with her.

"Amaryllis is a stupid computer freak," shouted John. "When I have Mr Mason for Driver's Ed on Friday, I'll have lots of time to tell him everything about the printer."

Amaryllis couldn't stay at the door, because she saw the teacher coming along. She walked into the angry group of teenagers. The conversation stopped suddenly and everybody hurried to sit down. The class were very quiet as Mrs Einstein, the Maths teacher, came in.

"I have something to tell those students from Mr Mason's homeroom. Somebody has repaired the broken computer printer he told you about yesterday. He's very pleased the problem is solved. Now please look at page 69 in your books."

Amaryllis felt all those eyes on the back of her head again, but this time she knew most of them were friendly. She found page 69. Now everybody knew Ms Norton was out of trouble for the moment.

Amaryllis couldn't wait to call her father. As soon as the last bell rung, she hurried to the phone outside the school and called him. "Daddy, have you repaired it?" she asked in a hurry.

"Well, we haven't finished. But we've found the problem. Your teacher can exchange the printers again tomorrow evening if everything goes all right."
"OK, Daddy. Thanks. See you tonight."
Then she ran back to school and across the courtyard to the G building.

In G116, Ms Norton was busy. She was printing some certificates for Games Day.
"How do you like them, Amaryllis?" she asked. She showed Amaryllis the sport certificates which looked really professional.
"They're beautiful! People will really like them." Amaryllis was enthusiastic. "Those different sports symbols are great. Each certificate will be special."
"Thanks. I'm glad you like them. I hope Mrs Jones likes them, too. Then maybe I'll feel strong enough to tell the truth when the school's printer is all right again."
Amaryllis didn't want Ms Norton to be unhappy any more. "Don't worry. They've found the problem. If everything goes well, you can exchange the printers tomorrow evening again." Amaryllis thought to herself, "And if John doesn't say anything to Mr Mason, I'll be out of trouble."
"OK. Call me as soon as you can. I'll come right over." Ms Norton seemed so happy that Amaryllis was glad she didn't know anything about John or what he was going to tell Mr Mason.

When the phone rang that evening, it was Carrot. So she told him she was worried about John. "Don't worry, Ammo," was Carrot's answer. "I'll talk to him."
"Well, thanks," she answered, "but my name is Amaryllis."
"Yeah, I know. But Amaryllis is too long. I'm glad you aren't afraid of old Mason and Big Mouth John. See you tomorrow. Bye."

"Thanks for calling. Bye." Ammo was the most terrible name Amaryllis could think of, but she was glad Carrot was on her side, too.

Chapter Four

On Thursday as soon as the last bell rang, Amaryllis ran to the phone again and called her father.

"Daddy?" She didn't even have to ask any questions.

"Everything is all right, Amaryllis," her father's friendly voice said. "Everything is working well. Tell Ms Norton that I'll be home by six."

"Thanks a million!" Amaryllis finished the shortest phone call of her life and ran back to the school building with the news. She didn't even check the coin return. Ms Norton was relieved.

"You're sure, aren't you, Amaryllis?" She wanted to be sure.

"Of course," laughed Amaryllis. "Any time after six at our house for the Second Great Printer Exchange. By tomorrow morning the school will have its printer back. Then it won't be important any more. You can tell Mrs Jones the truth and everything will be all right."

At six thirty that evening in the Craus' driveway, they exchanged the printers.

"I don't know how to thank you, Mr Craus. Amaryllis, would you like to drive over to school with me to bring this printer back? After all, it was your fantastic plan!"

"Sure. Is that OK, Dad?"

"Fine! See you later."

The school buildings were almost all dark. Ms Norton and Amaryllis were both happy as they carried the printer from

the car park to G116 and put it back in its place. "Home again," said Ms Norton, as she looked at the printer. "I won't move that again! At least not till Douglas is a few years older!"

They laughed as they walked back out of the building across the courtyard. "Computer companies should make their printers child-proof," said Amaryllis. They stopped laughing when they heard Mrs Jones, the head teacher, calling them. They turned to see her – she was hurrying behind them.

"Ah, um, good evening, Mrs Jones," Ms Norton said slowly. "I – um – I'm glad we've met. I have something to tell you."

"Now, I'm sure what I want to tell you is much more important," said Mrs Jones. "This afternoon, the Board of Education decided on the teaching jobs for next year. They agreed with us that you should get a new contract for next year. They want you to stay. We really like your work with the students. Also the extra time you spend on things outside the classroom and, well, like Games Day certificates!" Mrs Jones smiled.

Ms Norton didn't know what to say. "Thank you, Mrs Jones, thank you so much. I'll have to go home and tell my family."

"That's all right, Ms Norton. You've earned it."

As soon as Ms Norton drove her student home, Amaryllis went to the phone. First she called Sandy with the news about Ms Norton's future at the school. Then she called Carrot. "That's great, Ammo," said Carrot. "You really helped Ms Norton. Nobody else in the class was clever enough."

"That's OK," said Amaryllis. "I can't talk long now. My evening meal is on the table. See you tomorrow. Bye."

"Bye, Ammo. See you tomorrow."

"Maybe 'Ammo' isn't so bad after all," Amaryllis thought to herself. And John? Well, he just wasn't a problem any more.

When Amaryllis got back to the kitchen, she started to tell her parents about Ms Norton's contract, when the phone rang.

"I'll answer it," said Mr Craus. "You get some dinner."

"This is crazy," said Mrs Craus. "That phone hasn't stopped ringing for the last two evenings. This is worse than it was in Waltham!"

Waltham? Her old home in Waltham. It felt like a million years ago!

After the Stories ...

Jogging

A Words to do with sports

Jeff loves sports. Find the sports he practises.
Write all you can find about them
in the text.
Which other sports do you know?
Which sports do you and the pupils in your class practise?

B What's in a name?

You can use a person's name to describe them.
e.g. ***J*** *ogs every day*
E *njoys playing tennis*
F *inds out about a drug ring*
F *riends with Mike and Lucy*
Now do the same with ***BABS***, ***MIKE***, ***LUCY***.

C Very important people

Work with a partner.
Write the names of the people in the story.
Put the names in order with the most important first.
Choose four people who needn't be in the story.
Write a sentence to say why each person isn't important.

D Find the words. The letters in boxes give you another word from the text.

1. A voice said, "Fifty ❑ - - - - - - half an ounce."
2. The policeman said, "The law needs - ❑ - - - ."
3. On the Big Wednesday Jeff and Mike were - - - - - ❑ - .
4. Jeff was in the tenth ❑ - - - - .
5. Every - - ❑ - - - - - - Jeff went jogging.
6. Jeff clearly heard the word "- - - ❑ ".
7. Jeff's tennis - - ❑ - - was called Mr Allen.
8. The - - ❑ - - - - - - didn't believe Jeff.
9. The newspaper - ❑ - - - - - - asked a lot of questions.
10. Mike went to a - ❑ - - - - - school.

E Jeff started keeping notes about what they saw in Duncan Street.
Look at what they wrote in their diary on pages 10 and 11.
Work with a partner.
Write the diary for Wednesday, 28th November.
Compare your diaries.

F Look at page 16. The reporter of the 'Milford News' wanted to know everything that had happened.
The reporter asked a lot of questions.
Work with a partner.
Write a dialogue between the reporter and Mike and Jeff.
Record your dialogue on a cassette.
Compare your cassette dialogues.

G Look at the four pictures for the story.
Write a title for each picture.
Write a speech bubble for each person in each picture.

Amaryllis on Her Own

A Find all the words in the text that have to do with computers.
Compare your list with your partner's.
Perhaps you have a computer yourself and know more words.
Write five rules for the computer room.
e.g. *Don't touch the computer screens.*

B There are four chapters in the story.
Write a title for each chapter.

C Look at the list of adjectives.
Use them to describe Carrot, Mr Mason, etc. and/or some situations:
angry, busy, clever, crazy, friendly, loud, nice, noisy, sad, stupid, terrible, unhappy.
e.g. *Amaryllis feels unhappy when she hears that the printer is broken.*

D Who says it?
Find out who the persons are speaking to and what the situation is.

1. "Daddy, listen. This is an emergency."
2. "Ms Norton, Amaryllis is making mistakes in my program."
3. "Bye, Ammo. See you tomorrow."
4. "Amaryllis, tell the class something about yourself."
5. "This afternoon, the Board of Education decided on the teaching jobs for next year."
6. "Amaryllis, to tell you the truth, my son broke it."
7. "That's Michael, a terrible show-off."

E Find the words. The letters in boxes give you another word from the text.

1. Ms Norton has a two-year ❑ - - - - - - - .
2. Some of the pupils had to - ❑ - - together at one computer.
3. The computers are in a special - - - ❑ .
4. Mr Mason said the ❑ - - - - - of Allegiance in a bored voice.
5. There is a - ❑ - - - - - - - on new computers and printers.
6. John said, "Amaryllis is really in ❑ - - - - - - now."
7. Amaryllis phoned her father, "This is an - - ❑ - - - - - - ."
8. Amaryllis's father could ❑ - - - - - the broken printer.
9. Amaryllis comes from a small town near - - ❑ - - - .
10. Her father works at a computer ❑ - - - - - - .
11. Douglas broke the printer by - - - ❑ - - - - .
12. Amaryllis's - - - ❑ - - - - was H 212.
13. Michael often called his classmates "❑ - - - - - - - - - ".

14. Ms Norton always printed the ❑ - - - - - - - - - - -
for Games Day.
15. John thought that Amaryllis was
a computer - - ❑ - - .

F Do you remember the story well?

Work with a partner. Each choose a different chapter of the story.
Write it again with ten mistakes/changes.
Read it to your partner.
How many mistakes/changes can he/she find?

G Who is it? (X = he or she)

1. X shouted 'noodle head' at people.
2. X asked Amaryllis to tell the class about herself.
3. X teaches Maths.
4. X was in the computer room on Friday after school.
5. X broke the printer.
6. X has a two-year contract.
7. X repaired the printer.
8. X wanted to get Amaryllis into trouble.
9. X told Ms Norton that she would get a new contract for the next year.

H Work with a partner.

1. Which story do you like better?
2. Who is your favourite person in 'Jogging' and in 'Amaryllis on Her Own'?
3. Who is the funniest person in both stories?

4. Which person don't you like at all?
5. Collect the answers to 1 – 4 of all the pupils in your class.
   Write them on the board. Talk about your answers.
   e.g. *10 pupils think 'Jogging' is the best story.*
6. Find another title for the reader:
   – a new title with three words that begin with the same letter
   – a new title from a line in one of the stories
7. Look at the list of words.
   For each story, find 10 words which were important to you when you read it.
   Compare your lists.

List of Words

A **accident** ['æksɪdənt]: **by accident** zufällig
afraid [ə'freɪd]: **be afraid** sich fürchten
also ['ɔːlsəʊ] auch
anyway ['enɪweɪ] sowieso
around [ə'raʊnd] (her)um; **look around** sich umsehen
arrest [ə'rest] festnehmen
as far as [fɑː] bis
ask for [ɑːsk] bitten um
at least [ət 'liːst] mindestens
automatically [ɔːtə'mætɪklɪ] automatisch

B **back** [bæk] Rückseite
beard [bɪəd] Bart
beginning [bɪ'gɪnɪŋ] Anfang
believe [bɪ'liːv] glauben
bell [bel] Klingel
block [blɒk] blockieren, absperren
Board of Education [bɔːd əv edjʊ'keɪʃn] Schulbehörde
bother ['bɒðə] ärgern
bratty ['brætɪ] vorlaut; **her bratty self** vorlaut wie immer
brave [breɪv] mutig
breathe [briːð] atmen
business ['bɪznɪs] Geschäft; **away on business** geschäftlich unterwegs

C **car park** ['kaː paːk] Parkplatz
case [keɪs]: **in case** falls
catch, caught, caught [kætʃ,kɔːt] fangen; hängenbleiben
certificate [sə'tɪfɪkət] Zeugnis

change [tʃeɪndʒ] Veränderung
change back [tʃeɪndʒ] zurückstellen
cheer [tʃɪə] Beifall spenden, jubeln
child-proof ['tʃaɪld pruːf] kindersicher
clear [klɪə] klar, deutlich
clog [klɒg] verstopfen
coach [kəʊtʃ] Trainer(in)
coin return [kɔɪn rɪ'tɜːn] Münzrückgabe
coke [kəʊk] (*sl.* **cocaine** [kəʊ'keɪn]) „Koks“ (Kokain)
cold [kəʊld] Kälte
collect [kə'lekt] abholen
concentrate ['kɒnsəntreɪt] sich konzentrieren
confirm [kən'fɜːm] bestätigen
confused [kən'fjuːzd] verwirrt
congratulate [kən'grætʃʊleɪt] gratulieren
contract ['kɒntrækt] Vertrag
control [kən'trəʊl] Kontrolle; **take control of** überwältigen
conversation [kɒnvə'seɪʃn] Unterhaltung
convince [kən'vɪns] überzeugen
cool (*sl.*) [kuːl] „toll“
corner ['kɔːnə] Ecke
correct [kə'rekt] korrigieren
correct [kə'rekt] richtig; **be correct** recht haben
courtyard ['kɔːtjɑːd] Hof
crack [kræk] sprengen, zerbrechen
crazy ['kreɪzɪ] verrückt
criminal ['krɪmɪnl] Verbrecher(in)
criticize ['krɪtɪsaɪz] kritisieren

D **daughter** ['dɔːtə] Tochter
dealer ['diːlə] Händler(in)
decide [dɪ'saɪd] sich entschließen; **decide on** sich entscheiden für
deep [diːp] tief

department [dɪ'pɑːtmənt] Abteilung;
department head Fachleiter(in)
detail ['diːteɪl] Detail, Einzelheit
diary ['daɪərɪ] Tagebuch
dinner ['dɪnə] Abendessen
disappear [dɪsə'pɪə] verschwinden
discovery [dɪs'kʌvərɪ] Entdeckung
disguised [dɪs'gaɪzd] verkleidet
Driver's Ed = **Driver's Education** ['draɪvəz edjuː'keɪʃn] Fahrunterricht
driveway ['draɪvweɪ] Auffahrt
drugs [drʌgz] Drogen
during ['djʊərɪŋ] während
dynamic-looking [daɪ'næmɪk lʊkɪŋ] dynamisch aussehend

E **emergency** [ɪ'mɜːdʒənsɪ] Notfall
enthusiastic [ɪnθjuːzɪ'æstɪk] begeistert
escape [ɪ'skeɪp] fliehen, entkommen
especially ['ɪspeʃəlɪ] besonders
even though [iːvn 'ðəʊ] obwohl
evidence ['evɪdəns] Beweis(e)
exchange [ɪks'tʃeɪndʒ] austauschen; Austausch
eye [aɪ] Auge

F **face** [feɪs] Gesicht
fantasies ['fæntəsɪz] Phantastereien
fantastic [fæn'tæstɪk] phantastisch
fight [faɪt] kämpfen
finally ['faɪnəlɪ] endlich
follow ['fɒləʊ] folgen
for sale [fə 'seɪl] zu verkaufen
freak [friːk] Fanatiker(in)
frightening ['fraɪtnɪŋ] furchterregend
front page [frʌnt 'peɪdʒ] Titelseite

front seat [frʌnt ˈsiːt] Vordersitz
future [fjuːtʃə] Zukunft

G **Games Day** [ˈgeɪmz deɪ] Schulsportfest
gardener [ˈgɑːdnə] Gärtner(in)
gas [gæs] *AE* Benzin; **gas line** [ˈgæs laɪn] Benzinleitung
giggle [ˈgɪgl] kichern; Kichern
go on: what's going on? was ist los?
grade [greɪd] *AE* Jahrgangsstufe; **grades** Noten, Zensuren
grip [grɪp] Griff
gruff [grʌf] barsch, rauh
guarantee [gærənˈtiː] Garantie
guilty [ˈgɪltɪ] schuldig
guy [gaɪ] Kerl, Typ

H **hall** [hɔːl] Flur
head [hed] Kopf; **head teacher** Direktor(in)
helpless [ˈhelplɪs] hilflos
hero [ˈhɪərəʊ] Held
homeroom [ˈhəʊmrʊm] Klassenraum (*in dem sich die Klasse zum Unterrichtsbeginn versammelt)*
hurry [ˈhʌrɪ] eilen; **in a hurry** schnell

I **immediately** [ɪˈmiːdjətlɪ] sofort
involved [ɪnˈvɒlvd] verwickelt

J **jail** [dʒeɪl] Gefängnis
jog [dʒɒg] joggen; Lauf

K **keep, kept, kept** [kiːp, kept] (be)halten;
keep a diary ein Tagebuch führen;
keep busy beschäftigen
kit: tool kit [ˈtuːl kɪt] Werkzeugkasten

L **laser** ['leɪzə] Laser
last [lɑːst] reichen; dauern
lawn [lɔːn] Rasen
leather ['leðə] Leder
like a million dollars ['mɪljən 'dɒləz] wie im siebten Himmel
little ['lɪtl]: **a little** ein wenig
living-room ['lɪvɪŋ rʊm] Wohnzimmer
locker ['lɒkə] abschließbarer Schrank
look [lʊk]: **have a look at** ansehen
loss [lɒs] Niederlage
luckily ['lʌkɪlɪ] glücklicherweise
lunch ticket ['lʌntʃ 'tɪkɪt] Essenmarke

M **maybe** ['meɪbiː] vielleicht
measure ['meʒə] Maßnahme; **take measures** Maßnahmen ergreifen
menu ['menjuː] Speisekarte
microphone ['maɪkrəfəʊn] Mikrophon
mouth [maʊθ] Mund
move in [muːv] einziehen
mow [məʊ] mähen
Ms [mɪz] Frau *(familienstandneutrale Anrede)*

N **nearly** ['nɪəlɪ] beinahe, fast
neighbourhood ['neɪbəhʊd] Nachbarschaft, Wohngegend
none [nʌn] niemand, keine(r)
noodle ['nuːdl] Nudel; **noodle head** Strohkopf
not ... any more ['enɪ] nicht mehr
note [nəʊt] Notiz
now and then [ðen] hin und wieder

O **on and on** [ɒn ənd 'ɒn] immer weiter
on her own [əʊn] sich selbst überlassen;

once [wʌns] einmal; **for once** diesmal (ausnahmsweise)
ounce [aʊns] Unze *(28,35g)*
outside [aʊtˈsaɪd]: **on the outside** äußerlich
over and over again [ˈəʊvə ənd ˈəʊvə əˈgen] immer wieder; **all over again** noch einmal von vorn

P **paper bag** [ˈpeɪpə bæg] Tüte
pass [pɑːs] vorbeilaufen an; reichen
percentage [pəˈsentɪdʒ] Prozentzahl
photocopy [ˈfəʊtəʊkɒpɪ] Fotokopie
pie [paɪ] Pastete
pleased [pliːzd] erfreut
Pledge of Allegiance [pledʒ əv əˈliːdʒəns] Treuegelöbnis (*gegenüber der amerikanischen Nation*)
police officer [pəˈliːs ˈɒfɪsə] Polizeibeamter, -beamtin
popularity [pɒpjʊˈlærətɪ] Beliebtheit
possible [ˈpɒsəbl] möglich
practice [ˈpræktɪs] Training
printer [ˈprɪntə] Drucker
private school [ˈpraɪvɪt ˈskuːl] Privatschule
professional [prəˈfeʃənl] professionell, fachmännisch
program [ˈprəʊgræm] (Computer-)Programm; programmieren
proof [pruːf] Beweis(e)
pure [pjʊə] rein
pushed her way past [pʊʃt] drängte sich vorbei an

R **real** [rɪəl] echt
realize [ˈrɪəlaɪz] sich klarmachen
reason [ˈriːzn] Grund
record [ˈrekɔːd] Zeugnis
relieved [rɪˈliːvd] erleichtert
repairman [rɪˈpeəmən] Handwerker

repeat [rɪ'pi:t] wiederholen
reply [rɪ'plaɪ] erwidern
report [rɪ'pɔ:t] Zeugnis
result [rɪ'zʌlt] Ergebnis
right [raɪt] direkt; **right after** direkt danach;
right over genau gegenüber;
right up to bis dicht an
ring [rɪŋ]: **drug ring** Rauschgiftring
route [ru:t] Strecke
row [rəʊ] Reihe
run [rʌn] Lauf

S **scarf** [skɑ:f] Schal, Halstuch
screen [skri:n] Bildschirm
serious ['sɪərɪəs] ernsthaft
shadow ['ʃædəʊ] Schatten
share [ʃeə] sich teilen
short [ʃɔ:t] kurz; untersetzt
show-off ['ʃəʊ ɒf] Angeber(in)
side [saɪd] Seite
silence ['saɪləns] beruhigen
skate-board ['skeɪt bɔ:d] Skateboard fahren
solve [sɒlv] lösen
son [sʌn] (*hier*) Kleiner
spring [sprɪŋ] Frühling
stay after school [steɪ] länger in der Schule bleiben
stitch [stɪtʃ] Seitenstechen
strange [streɪndʒ] fremd
stranger ['streɪndʒə] Fremde(r)
substitute ['sʌbstɪtju:t] Ersatz-, Reservespieler(in)
such [sʌtʃ] solch(e, er, es)
surprise [sə'praɪz]: **by surprise** völlig überraschend
surprised [sə'praɪzd] überrascht

T **talk** [tɔːk] Rede, Ansprache; **give a talk** eine Rede halten
tape [teɪp] Tonband(aufnahme)
teaching job ['tiːtʃɪŋ dʒɒb] Lehrerstelle
technician [tek'nɪʃn] Techniker(in)
term [tɜːm] Schuljahr
therapy ['θerəpɪ] Therapie
thought [θɔːt] Gedanke
through [θruː] durch
tie [taɪ] binden
tool [tuːl] Werkzeug; **tool kit** Werkzeugkasten
trouble ['trʌbl] Schwierigkeit(en); **get into trouble** in Schwierigkeiten kommen
truth [truːθ] Wahrheit
try out [traɪ 'aʊt] an den Wettkämpfen teilnehmen

U **unclear** [ʌn'klɪə] undeutlich
unfriendly [ʌn'frendlɪ] unfreundlich
unhappy [ʌn'hæpɪ] unglücklich
unlikely [ʌn'laɪklɪ] unwahrscheinlich
unsure [ʌn'ʃʊə] unsicher

V **very first** ['verɪ 'fɜːst] allererst
voice [vɔɪs] Stimme

W **waste** [weɪst] verschwenden
while [waɪl] während
whisper ['wɪspə] flüstern; Flüstern
whistle ['wɪsl] pfeifen; Pfiff
whole [həʊl] ganz
win [wɪn] Sieg
wool [wʊl] Wolle
worried ['wʌrɪd] beunruhigt, unruhig

worth [wɜːθ] wert; **it isn't worth** es lohnt sich nicht
wrong [rɒŋ]: **go wrong** schiefgehen